T0363717

WRITERS

ON

WRITERS

Published in partnership with

STATE LIBRARY
VICTORIA
What's your story?

WRITERS
CHRISTOS TSIOLKAS
ON
PATRICK WHITE
WRITERS

Published by Black Inc.
in association with the University of Melbourne and State Library Victoria.

Black Inc., an imprint of Schwartz Publishing Pty Ltd
Level 1, 221 Drummond Street, Carlton VIC 3053, Australia
enquiries@blackincbooks.com • www.blackincbooks.com

State Library Victoria
328 Swanston Street, Melbourne VIC 3000, Australia
www.slv.vic.gov.au

The University of Melbourne
Parkville VIC 3010, Australia
www.unimelb.edu.au

9781863959797 (hardback)
9781743820483 (ebook)

A catalogue record for this
book is available from the
National Library of Australia

Cover and text design by Peter Long
Typesetting by Marilyn de Castro
Photograph of Christos Tsiolkas: Simon Schluter/Fairfax Media
Photograph of Patrick White: John Lamb/Fairfax Media

Printed in China by 1010 Printing.

In memoriam,
and with gratitude to,
Jaroslav Havir

Those who are doomed to become artists are seldom blessed with equanimity. They are tossed to drunken heights, only to be brought down into a sludge of headachy despair; their arrogance gives way to humiliation at the next curve of the switchback. This applies particularly to artists of the theatre. Most children have theatre in them. Those who carry it over into adolescence and, more or less, maturity, commit the ultimate indecency of becoming professional actors. If I didn't go all the way, I became instead that far more indecent hybrid, a frustrated one. Sexual ambivalence helped drive me in on myself. Lacking flamboyance, cursed with reserve, I chose fiction, or most likely it was chosen for me, as the means of introducing to a disbelieving audience the cast of contradictory characters of which I am composed.

– Flaws in the Glass

A QUESTION

I t is 2015 and I am on a panel at the Cheltenham Literature Festival in England alongside two other Australian writers, Bill Granger and Kathy Lette. The theme of our conversation is Australia itself, our culture and our writing, and, as so often happens when antipodeans try to make sense of "down under" for a British audience, the discussion is halting, superficial. I am sweating, uncomfortable onstage, aware that although there are so many things I want to say that are critical of my country – of our complacency, our parochialism, our immaturity in addressing the legacies of racism, our sordid and degrading contemporary politics – I am finding myself defensive, even antagonistic.

Not ten minutes ago, while trying to relax in the green room and getting to know my fellow panellists, I had been reciting silently to myself the list of negatives that I felt duty-bound to convey to the audience. But now, in front of the crowd, I am struggling to make myself understood. I am happy to rant against my nation, but I don't want these Europeans to lord it over us, me, we Australians on the stage. I want *their* continent to take responsibility for the colonial history that spawned us. But I hear myself sounding petulant and feel guilty that I am undermining the good humour of my fellow panellists. I can almost pick up the murmur from the crowd: *That Aussie sure has a chip on his shoulder.*

It's during question time that a member of the audience throws me a lifeline. Christos, what do Australians think of Patrick White these days? he asks. And now my response is immediate and sure. I have only just finished reading White's *The Tree of Man* and the writing remains vivid, as if grafted to my memory. I express as best as I can how deeply affected I have been by the novel, that it accomplishes so much of what we writers wish to do and so seldom achieve: the power and intensity of timelessness. It is, I say, one of the great novels, and my statement doesn't require the qualification of that lousy adjective "Australian". It is one of the great works of literature. And although I disavow the need for the qualifier, the scents and sounds, the speech and syntax, the brutality and beauty of my continent permeates the writing. I can't answer for all Australians, I conclude by saying, but I do feel a certain shame that it has taken me so long to come to this book.

I don't think my answer satisfied him.

Months after returning home, I find myself going back to the man's question, to puzzle over it and try to make sense of it. By now I am completely immersed in White's writing. On New Year's Eve I had made a resolution to spend all of 2016 reading the man's work. Before this, I had tried to read *Voss* in high school, and as a young man had read *The Twyborn Affair*. I had seen a production of White's play *The Ham Funeral* and I had read his short stories. Also while in high school, I had watched the film *The Night the Prowler*, scripted by White and directed by Jim Sharman. (I maintain that the film is criminally neglected to this day.)

So it wasn't that White was unknown to me, nor that I bore him any particular resentment or suspicion. But by the end of 2016 I knew that the man had written three of the greatest novels of the twentieth century: *The Tree of Man*, *The Solid Mandala* and *The Eye of the Storm*. In saying this, I don't mean to diminish the strengths and ravishing literary eloquence of *Voss*, *Riders in the Chariot*, *The Vivisector* and *The Twyborn Affair*, which I also believe to be great works. But there are novels that in the reading enact a transformation that sees their characters and language become part of oneself, that literally change the way you look upon the world. If you are both a reader *and* a writer, then this transformation initiates the alchemy of inspiration; the structure that a great writer employs – their discipline, their control – and their fierce will to tell a story and create an imaginary world that resonates with the reality the reader inhabits, will inevitably become part of the way you wish to tell your own stories and will influence the way you conjure your own imaginary worlds. Reading a great writer is a challenge because it always makes you want to better yourself.

I wish I had it in me to write an epic such as *The Tree of Man*. I am grateful to *The Solid Mandala* for reminding me that the suburban and the quiet can be as transcendent and inspiring as the cosmopolitan and the calamitous. As for *The Eye of the Storm*, I find it inconceivable to write again about family without thinking of how the structure of that novel allows characters to sing individually, contrapuntally, and also as essential components of a whole. So I *am* ashamed that it took me so long to come to this understanding of Patrick White. And also pissed off: why didn't my tutors, my fellow writers and our critics make sure I got there earlier?

This sense of pissed-offness is the reason I agreed to write this book. The question the man asked me in Cheltenham was not disconnected from the halting conversation we were having onstage about what it means to be Australian and how such meanings influence the kind of writing we do. Patrick White, winner of the Nobel Prize in Literature, is arguably the most eminent of Australian writers, but I was able to work for close to two decades as a writer without feeling either the need or the desire to engage with his work.

As a man and as a reluctant public intellectual, Patrick White was vitriolic in his contempt for so many aspects of Australian culture. But he was also unusual in refusing the siren song of expatriation that seemed irresistible to so many artists of his generation. And he was a white man, not merely of settler origins but a member of the "squattocracy". This must have played a part in my cavalier disregard of his work. I made the assumption that he was one of the "dead white males", a judgement bolstered by the postmodern, anti-canonical, feminist and postcolonial criticism that was beginning to dominate literary criticism and the academy in the 1980s, when I was a university student. That was, of course, the question beneath the question, the *real* question, that the man from the audience was posing: What does Patrick White's work mean to us now? Does it still speak to us? In trying to answer this, I don't want to lose sight of the greater objective of this book, which is to honour the writing itself. But to do that, I have to continue to wrestle with the question of how White speaks to us in the present.

SMYRNA

When I read David Marr's commanding biography, *Patrick White: A Life*, the storyteller in me was delighted to find that the young Patrick had been shipped to Cheltenham College in England as a youth, and that there he had experienced an exile from home and family that marked his character and his writing throughout his life. Marr eloquently describes the alienation the young boy felt upon being wrenched from his privileged and cocooned upbringing in rural New South Wales and bourgeois Sydney, to find himself suddenly a colonial misfit in one of the elite centres of English life.

I found myself in Cheltenham over seventy years later, and while there said to a friend, My God, this is one of the whitest places I've ever been. Something of the strangeness I felt in Cheltenham, the sense of being an outsider, made sense to me when I read Marr's account of White's experience as a schoolboy. This is precisely where the storyteller in me gets excited.

Of course, life isn't fiction and it would be reckless to presume that the confusions and emotions the young Patrick White experienced as a transplanted colonial in Cheltenham eighty or more years ago were identical to the discombobulating anxiety I experienced as an Australian writer visiting the UK in the early twenty-first century. For one, White came from a line of wealthy Australian landholders and was born into a family that proudly asserted its British origins. I was born to peasant Greek immigrants whose migration to Australia made our family very much part of the working class. Nevertheless, despite these differences of time, history and cultural roots, there is something in White's attraction to, and resentment of, his colonial status that links him to me.

White railed against the parochialism and mean-spiritedness of Australian culture all his life and this antagonism is a constant presence in his writing. It lends his wonderful autobiography, *Flaws in the Glass*, some of its most vivid imagery. And a fractious desire – fractious because never fulfilled, never finally consummated – to leave Australia and make Europe his permanent home is part of the life that Marr surveyed and also a recurrent desire of the characters in White's novels. In fiction he could satisfy that longing: in both the early work, *An Aunt's Story*, and in the late masterpiece, *The Twyborn Affair*, main characters can make that great divorce.

But White himself remained in Australia till the end of his life. That in itself is an important biographical element that I think informs how we understand his work. The flight of mid-twentieth-century writers from Australia in order to consolidate their identities and their careers was so commonplace as to be unremarkable – so much so that we had a name for the sense of inferiority involved: "cultural cringe". Randolph Stowe and Christina Stead, two other writers of comparable ability, had to leave their home country to continue writing. And a later generation that includes Robert Hughes, Germaine Greer and Clive James also had to make that particular migration. I think one thing that marks White's writing and makes it different from the work of these other writers is that the Australia that emerges across his work is not static. This country, in all its beauty and ugliness, in all its meanness and potential, is a perpetual character in his novels. It changes and grows, it keeps repeating the same mistakes, and yet it can surprise us. This is one of the things I adore about the man's work. There isn't a whiff of nostalgia for Australia in his writing.

David Marr's biography and *Flaws in the Glass* are such definitive works on Patrick White's life and imagination that we might believe there to be no further call for biographical excavation, that they provide all the illumination we need. But I want to offer another work as also pivotal to our understanding of White. This is a lesser-known book by the critic and academic Vrasidas Karalis, his *Recollections of Mr Manoly Lascaris*. Published in 2008 and based on a series of interviews Karalis conducted with Lascaris, Patrick White's long-term partner, the book is of interest not only for the insights it provides into White and his relationship with Lascaris, but also as an honest reflection by Karalis on the existential impermanence of the migrant experience.

The Lascaris who emerges from these conversations scuttles the romantic and clichéd sense of him as immigrant and refugee that I had been carrying around in my head for years. Of course, there is political and historical tragedy in his biography, specifically the almost complete purge of the Greek, Armenian and Jewish communities in Anatolia after the creation of the modern Turkish state in the early 1920s. Lascaris's family, who lived in the Ottoman city of Smyrna (now Izmir), had to flee the city and were scattered, as were hundreds of thousands of other refugees, across Europe, Egypt, Canada and the USA. But Lascaris is clear in wishing to distinguish his own family's experience from that of peasant and working-class Anatolian refugees.

As they converse, the older man admonishes the younger for "proletarian" and "vulgar" expressions. The use of that specifically Marxist term "proletarian" is telling, as if Lascaris wishes to place himself outside the familiar sociopolitical understanding of migration. His isn't the confession of a "wog", he seems to be implying, and in so doing he marks a gulf between his own experience and that of the overwhelming majority of Greek immigrants. Lascaris is proud of his family's connection to the royal court of ancient Byzantium; he is, whatever the realities of his bank account, always an aristocrat.

Hearing Lascaris's voice in his interviews with Karalis, I am granted insight into a very different perception to that of the Greek emigrants I grew up among, where the dominant narratives spoke of grinding rural poverty and limited education, experiences that owed nothing to and had no relationship with cosmopolitan, urban centres. I think it is in understanding that difference that I gleaned how much White and Lascaris shared in their comprehension of exile. One Australian and the other Anatolian, they were both upper-class men who owed allegiance to an idea of Empire. In fact, that's how they met – both fighting in a world war wearing British uniforms. But that allegiance was also challenged, and therefore in part resented, because the very notion of Empire was collapsing, and the Britain they belonged to either condescended to them or no longer wanted them. This alienation from Empire they also shared.

The one thread that connects Lascaris to the Greece I know from my family history, and one of the great gifts Manoly bestowed on his lover, is the religion of Greek Orthodoxy. From his interviews, it becomes clear that Lascaris's devout faith cannot be divorced from his pride in the history of the religion. Faith is both belief *and* blood. For the Greeks living in Anatolia and the Middle East, it was their religion, even more than their language, that set them apart from their neighbours. But if that was all religion meant to Lascaris, it would not have had the impact it did on White as a writer.

Greek Orthodoxy's history, separated by schism and Empire from Western Europe, surviving for half a millennium in a largely Muslim world, is characterised by mysteries that exhort the unknowability of God. Cleaved from earthly power with the conquest of Constantinople by the Ottomans, Orthodoxy is marked by a fatalism that separates it from both Catholicism and Protestantism. Orthodoxy's lore reifies the seer, the hermit and the seeker, those who abandon earthly pleasures to find God's immanence in the natural world. Orthodoxy eschews the intellectual quest for God.

It's not faith that Patrick White takes from Orthodoxy, but a *sensibility*, one that allowed him to return to Australia and see the landscape in a way he could not before his relationship with Manolis. The seer, the hermit and the seeker will become central to his work, and the spirituality in his novels will not arise from characters pondering the existence or non-existence of a deity, but from encountering the Godhead in the violences and ecstasies of the natural world. It's this sensibility that connects White's writing, for me, to the great Russian writers. It is this supreme gift that I think Lascaris gave him.

I suspect an intervention is necessary here, that I may need to defend myself against the accusation that it is my own Greek heritage that steers me towards Lascaris and his influence on White. This is true, undoubtedly. But I ask you to trust that what I am trying to get at is a transformation in White's writing that is linked to his falling in love with Manoly Lascaris – that by falling in love and pledging a commitment to a life together, White took on an understanding of exile and of spirituality that was bestowed on him by his lover.

Of course, White's feelings of being an outsider to his country and family heritage were already there before World War II and before meeting Manoly. As he points out in *Flaws in the Glass*, "Sexual ambivalence helped drive me in on myself." Those outsider emotions were there during his time as a schoolboy in Cheltenham, and then later when he returned to the UK after spending time as a jackeroo in outback New South Wales. The rage and the hopelessness he felt at the paradoxical smallness of Australia, that incredible smallness of such a huge country, find expression in *The Happy Valley*, his first novel. And, in his second, *The Living and the Dead*, a book that betrays the urgency of a young writer trying to prove he is the equal of the European writers who have influenced him, Australia is almost – almost, but not quite – excluded.[1] But undoubtedly, although the first two novels confirm the young White as an immensely talented writer, they pale alongside the novels he was to write on his return to Australia, with Manoly, after the war.

There is an alertness to beauty and to the sensuality of landscape in *The Happy Valley* and there is also an awareness of the vastness and sometimes bleakness of space. But there is no awe. What I miss in this book and in *The Living and the Dead* are the flights of ecstatic lyricism that are so much part of the experience of reading *The Aunt's Story* (first published in 1948), *The Tree of*

---

1   In later life White was dismissive of *The Happy Valley*, a dismissal I can't avow. I think the novel is redolent of rural life, its language translating the colours and hues of the landscape, the smells and sounds of the Australian bush. And it does something more: the almost raw evocation of the sensuality of the bush is in constant contrast to the repression and quiet desperation that affect most of the characters.

Man (1955) and *Voss* (1957). Yes, that difference can be attributed to the maturing of the man through his experience of life in England and, crucially, to his experience as a soldier in war. And by the time of *The Aunt's Story* White had gained a confidence in his craft that saw him begin to transcend his modernist influences. Yet what also emerges across these three great early works is a defiant celebration of the wanderer, the exile and the pilgrim; and also a spiritual dimension to his writing, a language of transcendence that finds the sacred in the material world and in the accidental moments when strangers bestow kindness on one another.

White's notion of the sacred is never sentimental; nor is his championing of the exile. A suspicion of madness and self-delusion taints the revelatory bliss of *The Aunt's Story*'s Theodora Goodman, as it does the gargantuan folly of explorer Johann Ulrich Voss. And in *The Tree of Man*, Stan and Amy Parker are Adam and Eve before the Fall, though this innocence and grace is apprehended by them only in blinding moments of illumination that last an instant; it is certainly not understood by their children and the community that begins to form around their once isolated farm. But madness, folly and naivety do not diminish any of these characters. Their vividness is a transcendence that we as readers comprehend and are shaken by.

This is the foundation of my love for Patrick White. And I believe that this foundation is inseparable from the gifts that Lascaris offered his partner: a fierce and life-long commitment to the experience of exile suffered by the displaced Anatolians, and an understanding and love for the material spiritualism of Greek Orthodoxy that offered a way for White to create a language of spiritual yearning and devotion, even as an avowed non-believer. The Orthodox East enters White's writing and this is transformative, not only for his language, but also for how it initiates something in Australian literature. What I am trying to do is to convey something of the wonder I experienced as both reader and writer in finding White, at first tentatively and then with greater confidence, creating an immigrant language.

> *'Greece, you see, is a bare country. It is all bones.'*
>
> *'Like Meroe,' said Theodora.*
>
> *'Please?' said Moraïtis.*
>
> *'I too come from a country of bones.'*
>
> *'That is good,' said Moraïtis solemnly. 'It is easier to see.'*
>
> – The Aunt's Story

A comparison between *The Living and the Dead* and *The Aunt's Story* is instructive for teasing out the new directions that White would take as a writer after World War II. A study of a brother and sister whose pampered bourgeois existence is increasingly called into question following the Great War and then the social and political upheavals in Europe of the 1920s and 1930s, the earlier novel is arguably a more elegant work. The writing is poised, even as the young writer uses the modernist technique of stream of consciousness to achieve his effects. In *The Living and the Dead*, the centre of the world, the centre of the very universe, is Europe and more specifically London. And the language, the syntax, the characters and the world are all English. I mean by this that even the hints of the Australian vernacular of *The Happy Valley* – a sharpness, a harshness – are gone.

Read now, after the passing of so many decades, *The Living and the Dead* seems a consummate young person's novel from the 1930s, and though that means reading it is pleasurable, it is also quite unremarkable. It is as if White as a young man had begun that trajectory that was to be enacted again and again by so many of his contemporaries – of preparing for a life as an English writer by putting the place of his birth behind him. Reading it now, knowing where his life and his writing were to take him, I can't help but offer a small prayer to the gods that he was dissuaded from pursuing this course. On the evidence of this novel White could have been a perfectly fine English writer. It is as an *Australian* writer – and as an Australian writer seeing both his country and the world partly through Lascaris's eyes – that he achieves greatness.

If *The Living and the Dead* seems precise and studied in what it wants to achieve – to be English – White's next novel, *The Aunt's Story*, stuns in the delirium of its writing and, sometimes, the incoherence of its story. It was the first of his novels that I read, back in my youth, and I will be honest: it dumbfounded me. I had to force myself to return to it. Yet I learnt a lesson that has remained with me ever since: to read passages aloud, to trust my ear to give me access to the language first, before my intellect and consciousness. And that was how, in a small room in a share house, leaping from my bed and holding the book to the dawn light, I first surrendered to White's writing. By chanting the sentences in this way I came to understand that there was an ecstasy to the writing, that in following Theodora Goodman's unravelling, from her journey first to Europe and then to the USA, we as readers were embarking alongside her on a journey into a strange new world, one where both Australia and Europe were rendered slightly ridiculous.

White's sensuality, which was only hinted at in *The Happy Valley*, begins to emerge more fully in this book. Something more important than geography was being discovered in the very writing. The choice is no longer the simple one of choosing to be Australian or choosing to be European. Theodora, the transplanted Australian, becomes the émigré pilgrim, her status as a visionary arising from her acceptance of the grace and gift of being an outsider in her worlds. The radical insight we discover as readers, and that continues to make *The Aunt's Story* such a revelatory work, is that it doesn't matter if Theo's visions arise from madness and the disintegration of self. They are real for her and they distil something of what it is to be the stranger in the world. Naïve, snobbish, lost and unsophisticated, Theodora may not be the most ideal of migrant heroes, but a hero is what she is. The novel speaks from within the experience of being outside. It could have been titled *The Migrant's Story*. This is the ecstasy that I gleaned only in snatches back in my youth, the song that I now recognise, re-reading *The Aunt's Story* in middle age, as the song of the wanderer.

She would have touched her head and said: Theodora I shall tell you the truth. Probably you will never marry. We are not the kind. You will not say the things they want to hear, flattering their vanity and their strength, because you will not know how, instinctively, and because it would not flatter you. But there is much that you will experience. You will see clearly, beyond the bone.

You will grow up probably ugly, and walk through life in sensible shoes. Because you are honest, and because you are barren, you will be both honoured and despised. You will never make a statue, nor write a poem. Although you will be torn by the agonies of music, you are not creative. You have not the artist's vanity, which is moved finally to express itself in its objects. But there will be moments of passing affection, through which the opaque world will become transparent, and of such a moment you will be able to say – my dear child.

– The Aunt's Story

This is the new element in White's achievement. To trace for the first time, to be among the earliest to express, in the English language, the migrant's story.

The literary politics of the early twenty-first century make such a claim audacious, even scandalous – for isn't White as white as his name? – but the truth is that White's achievements, in the rush of writing that coincides with his return to Australia, transcend the bounds of identity. From *The Aunt's Story* onwards he will write as woman, as Aborigine, as Jew, as migrant, and always as outsider. What these transformations allow for readers, too, is the leap of faith that is the great gift of the novel form – the licence to imagine ourselves in completely different guises and genders and experiences. And for those of us who are writers, White's work dares us to resurrect this capacity of the novel even as we are increasingly aware of how the novel's emergence from within European history makes the universalism of such a claim now suspect. Here I think it is no accident that White is a colonial subject, Australian, not from the centre. I think what initiates this great audacity – this ability to imagine and speak in so many voices, from within so many experiences – is the pledging of his life to Manolis Lascaris, refracting his own experiences of exile and of being an outsider through those of his immigrant lover; and discovering, also through Lascaris, a spiritual language with which to communicate.

I am trying to get at what it is in the man's work that means so much to me, and why I believe White's writing should not be consigned to literary history or confined to the twentieth century. I hope it is clear that I am not suggesting that White was merely translating what he learnt from Lascaris. The audacity, the wonder, comes from the new Australian language that White created to express this understanding. This daring, this verve, offers Australian writers a way of persisting to write outside ourselves and to commit to the novel, not only as a form of the past but also as a form of the present and for the future. And because White's achievements exceed the categories of nationhood and geography – he is both a great Australian novelist and a great novelist *period* – his legacy is an inspiration for a novelist wherever she might find herself.

Just the other month, I was corresponding with a writer friend from the Philippines who was struggling with the question of how to write a multi-character novel that could illuminate something of her country's complex and tumultuous colonial history. I suggested she read White's *The Eye of the Storm*. She wrote back with enthusiasm and joy at having discovered a novel that could explicate a world – and make sense of our world – in the form of a chamber piece: how White can make history comprehensible out of the interconnections and violent disruptions of family life. Her email thrilled me. We don't have to abandon the novel. There was something intimate in that thrill, the passing on of a love. Please, I urged her, please read *The Tree of Man* next.

Two people do not lose themselves at the identical moment, or else they might find each other, and be saved. It is not as simple as that.

– The Tree of Man

The adamantly secular will scoff but there does seem to be something of the miraculous in *The Tree of Man*. The critical third eye that is always present when I read, that clocks the not-quite-right word or the lazy sentence, the unnecessary exposition or lugubrious description even within the books I cherish, the books I adore and which I think are tremendous – that eye is of no use when I read *The Tree of Man*. There are a handful of novels that have had this effect on me: Austen's *Pride and Prejudice*, Tolstoy' *Anna Karenina*, Woolf's *The Waves*, Tanizaki's *The Makioka Sisters*, Ellison's *Invisible Man*, Nabokov's *Lolita*, Yourcenar's *Memoirs of Hadrian*, Endō's *Scandal* and Rushdie's *Midnight's Children*. (Even as I glance at this list I am all too aware that it doesn't include the writers and the books that mean the most to me, novels that I love possibly more than the ones I have listed above: no Dostoevsky, no Conrad, no Stendhal, no Genet, no Mailer and no Céline.)

The miracle of these perfect novels is that, from the opening sentence to the final word, the real world collapses and we are enfolded in a fictional reality that is stronger and more present than our material surroundings. The gift of being enraptured by such novels is that they continue to feed our desire as readers, to keep us hungrily reading, greedily searching for that experience once more. That the experience is so rare doesn't invalidate or contaminate the reading we do when we are searching. We keep reading, even if we are often disappointed, because as maturing readers we realise that there are also pleasures to be found in those novels that don't quite work. We still fall in love with novels and with writing, we are forgiving of imperfection, banality, pedestrian syntax. This is intrinsic to the erotics of reading.

And also to the erotics of writing. In no way do I want to diminish the necessity of discipline and the labour of craft that is essential to the writing of a novel. I am suspicious of a romantic notion of literary genius. Writing is work. But once transfigured by reading a work such as *The Tree of Man*, by the realisation that it is beyond one's calling to imagine and then write such a novel, you are not incapacitated as a writer. Rather, you are humbled, and your return to the desk is tempered by this understanding. You are grateful for the opportunity that life and circumstances have given you to engage in your labour. You are careful from then on, as I am now after reading *The Tree of Man*, to watch against self-regard, to fight against turpitude, and to accept but also confront your own limitations. Your approach from now on is that of the besotted, grateful and self-disciplined lover of literature.

After *The Tree of Man*, this is how much I love Patrick White, as a reader and as a writer. And this is an Australian novel, this is an Australian book. It came from within our immature and too often inward-looking culture. That too feels a little miraculous.

Then the man took an axe and struck the side of
a hairy tree, more to hear the sound than for any
other reason. And the sound was cold and loud.
The man struck at the tree, and struck, till several
white chips had fallen. He looked at the scar in the
side of the tree. The silence was immense. It was
the first time anything like this had happened in
that part of the bush.

— The Tree of Man

Stan and Amy Parker, the protagonists of *The Tree
of Man*, are a couple who create a home and a farm
in the rural wilderness. They are humble persons,
neither educated nor privileged, and their daily
existence is at the mercy of the savagery of nature,
the callousness of the climate and the isolation
of their environment. By the time they reach the
end of their lives, their small home is soon to
be encroached upon by the ever-expanding city.
In the end, death, which they have been conscious
of throughout their lives — for it is ever-present

in the wildness that they have tentatively tried, without success, to tame – comes for them.

The blurb of my Penguin edition refers to the novel as "a genesis story", which is apt because it is an origin story for the generations of settlers and migrants who have come to Australia seeking to create a new life. In saying this, I am conscious of what the novel is not and cannot be, which is a foundation story for the first peoples of this country. Those stories were not White's to tell. There is an argument to be had that in ignoring that central condition of being Australian – the relationship and history of the Aborigine and the settler – White maintained the great and ugly silence about race relations in our country. Indeed, soon after *The Tree of Man*, Randolph Stow published *To the Islands* (1958) and *Tourmaline* (1965), two pivotal novels about the crisis of guilt and responsibility that is part of each and every non-Indigenous Australian's inheritance in coming to personhood as an Australian. And already in 1929 Katharine

Susannah Prichard had published *Coonardoo*, her great novel about the impossible love between a white man and an Aboriginal woman – impossible because of the European man's failure of empathy and courage. The responsibility of addressing the Aboriginal experience, not only as history and as contemporary reality, but also as a question of how to write in an Australian English, would be taken up by White in his two subsequent novels, *Voss* and *Riders in the Chariot*.

And yet, *The Tree of Man* is not compromised by this silence. Its meaning and force are not to be found in its being some kind of Urtext of Australian history, but in being one of the first great novels to be written about the migrant experience in the English language. That Amy and Stan Parker are not immigrants as we now define them doesn't mitigate the immense accomplishment of the novel.

I wish to purposefully unite two terms that continue to be separated in Australian culture – "settlers" and "migrants". I believe one of White's achievements is to link the pioneer experience of White Australia to the general history of migration to this country. To be sure, the specifically British colonial history of Australia means that we understand the "settler" to be English-speaking while the "migrant" is from a non-English-speaking background, but what is revelatory for me as a reader of *The Tree of Man* is that the "Englishness" of Stan and Amy is inconsequential. It is precisely this imaginative and therefore historic leap taken by White that means I read the book as the first great migrant story in our literary culture. To be blunt, when reading the book I could see my mother and my father in the characters. I know this perspective might be deemed controversial or eccentric but there is no Australian novel previous to *The Tree of Man* that I have read in which this is a possibility.

The important question to ask here is not whether Stan and Amy are settlers or immigrants, but rather how White achieved this blurring and subversion of the distinction. In part, I think, it is because White creates a symbolic language of terrain and isolation, and it is this imaginative rendering of the condition of exile, conveying a migrant's continuing experience of dislocation through Stan and Amy's encounters with the natural world, that makes the novel so resonantly compelling, so continuously relevant. If their surname marks the Parkers as having an English heritage, the language of the novel, its almost animist expression of the spirituality to be found in rituals of labour and dedication to land, is a language that speaks across cultures, fusing the relationship to work, land and place shared by both settlers and migrants.

That is a truth that unites migrant cultures across the globe: the move from "homelessness" and estrangement to "settlement" and the coming to terms with exile is accomplished through labour, through the raising of children on soil that was once foreign but with the child's first step is indelibly marked as a new home. This doesn't always assuage the pain of exile, but it sometimes does, and what is profound in *The Tree of Man* is that through the different experiences of Stan and Amy we glimpse both possibilities.

In this sense, because migration is now one of the key shared experiences of people across the globe, *The Tree of Man* is a folk tale, and its language and expression are not beholden to Anglophone culture. On first reading it, the comparisons I made were not to previous Australian novels – even though the depicted light, soil and earth are so very much the elemental forces of this continent – but to Tolstoy and Kazantzakis. The novel centres on a remarkable moment of spiritual transcendence that Stan Parker experiences. God doesn't speak to him, but he senses God in the silence.

The man who was watching the storm, and who seemed to be sitting right at the centre of it, was at first exultant. Like his own dry paddocks, his skin drank the rain. He folded his wet arms, and this attitude added to his complacency. He was firm and strong, husband, father, and owner of cattle. He sat there touching his own muscular arms, for he had taken off his shirt during the heat and was wearing his singlet. But as the storm increased, his flesh had doubts, and he began to experience humility. The lightning, which could have struck open basalt, had, it seemed, the power to open souls. It was obvious in the yellow flash that something like this had happened, the flesh had slipped from his bones, and a light was shining in his cavernous skull.

– The Tree of Man

The *Tree of Man* is a genesis story, in the sense that every narrative of exile and migration is founded on the creation of oneself anew in a "new world". But a more apt comparison might be to the masterwork

created by the anonymous writers and compil-
ers of the Book of Job. Certainly the tragedies
and deprivations visited on the Parkers are not
as catastrophic as those suffered by Job, but Amy
and Stan contend with poverty, drought, flood
and illness and they must continue to husband
a land that everywhere announces the presence
of God, even if that God never makes Himself
knowable. Written after World War II and the
dawning awareness of the terrible immensity of
the Holocaust – an awareness that would lead
White to write his most avowedly "political" novel,
Riders in the Chariot – the spirituality of *The Tree
of Man* is existential and deist even as it borrows
from Judaism and Christianity.

I suspect that one of the reasons the novel has,
for such a long period, met with a great silence in
Australia is precisely its spiritual cogency. I was not
taught it in high school and it was not a book that
featured on the reading lists of my undergraduate
study. Deconstructive and materialist readings

have little to offer to the understanding of such a novel. Postmodernism shared with neoliberalism the arrogant assumption that they were modes of thinking that inaugurated the end of history. Yet history didn't end with the end of the Cold War and people are still seeking knowledge and joy and challenge and astonishment from books. All the questions have not been asked, let alone answered.

I think that both White and *The Tree of Man* have survived the postmodernists' sullen disregard. *Every* migrant and *every generation* of immigrant must engage in the labour of re-creation – just as they must come to an understanding of perpetual exile even as they toil in the construction of their new home, making their garden anew. The work, the language, the astounding literary power of this novel belongs to White. Its insight and understanding, its astounding *spiritual* power, is, I think, shared by White and Lascaris.

SARSAPARILLA

Castle Hill, thirty kilometres northwest of Sydney's CBD, is now very much part of Sydney suburbia, but when Patrick White and Manoly Lascaris moved there in 1948 it was still a largely rural community. They purchased a small farm, growing flowers and vegetables to sell, as well as breeding dogs (hence "Dogwoods", their name for the property). Financially the farm was a failure. But Castle Hill was the inspiration for some of White's most splendid writing, in novels, short stories and plays.

White will rename Castle Hill "Sarsaparilla". It's an inspiring choice, a masterful choice – so evocative of place that I recall trying to find it on a map of New South Wales when I was a young adult, after I first read White's short stories. It is in Castle Hill that he will write the great suite of works, from *The Tree of Man* to *The Solid Mandala*, that will cement his reputation as a novelist. Sarsaparilla will also be the setting for the caustic comedy of his plays *A Night in Sarsaparilla* and *A Cheery Soul.*

White's abrasive self-presentation, his patrician disdain for the bourgeoisie and his constant denunciations of the "giant emptiness" of Australia and Australians, have had an effect on how we perceive Sarsaparilla. This is a persona that he came to cultivate increasingly in his public pronouncements, culminating in the deeply cutting voice of *Flaws in the Glass.* So it is always a kind of shock to return to the writing itself and discover anew that there is great humanity and warmth in the fictional worlds he created.

It will be in *The Solid Mandala* that the town of Sarsaparilla takes centrestage, where White will most elegantly and poignantly suggest that within this most suburban of locales there are people living lives of piercing integrity alongside the ugly hypocrites of aspirational social climbing and conventional morality. In this novel, White will achieve again that astounding miracle of writing a book of which I can't imagine changing a single word, a novel that is a deliriously exquisite song from the very beginning to the very end, a novel that inspires me to dare the risk of humanism. I am deliberate in choosing that word "risk", because in our contemporary moment the universalism embodied in Enlightenment philosophies is under constant – and sometimes justified – attack. That fractious Hydra of representational politics – lop off one head, be it gender, race, nation, sexuality, and another identity emerges swiftly to take its place – makes the classical virtues of the novel, the protagonist as Every*man* and the verity of eternal truths, increasingly untenable. For those of us writing now, is it possible to believe anymore that a novel can speak to all?

But written at a time when such critiques were only beginning to arise, White's novel is a reminder that great fiction can escape the temporal fetters of culture and history to resonate and move us collectively long after the fact.

I am not going to temper this statement or apologise for it: I think any serious and hungry reader will be elated by *The Solid Mandala* wherever in the world she is, and whatever her circumstances. We readers who are also writers or artists will recognise ourselves in the Brown twins, in the purity of expression that is Arthur and in the compromise and pettiness of aspiration that is Waldo. And even if we are atheists, we must recognise – for the title announces it – that this is one of the great novels of spiritual meaning.

Where did such a book come from? What makes such a book possible? To try to answer that, I have to return to the books that preceded *The Solid Mandala*, to *Voss* and, most pertinently, *Riders in the Chariot*.

By its radiance, he did finally recognise her
face, and would have gone to her, if it had been
possible, but it was not; his body was worn out.

Instead, she came to him, and at once he was
flooded with light and memory. As she lay beside
him, his boyhood slipped from him in a rustling
of water and a rough towel. A steady summer had
possessed them. Leaves were in her lips, that he
bit off, and from her breast the full, silky, milky
buds. They were holding each other's heads and
looking into them, as remorsefully as children
looking at secrets, and seeing all too clearly.
But unlike children, they were confronted to
recognise their own faults.

So they were growing together, and loving. No
sore was so scrofulous on his body that she would
not touch it with her kindness. He would kiss
her wounds, even the deepest ones, that he had
inflicted himself and left to suppurate.

Given time, the man and woman might have healed each other. That time is not given was their one sadness. But time itself is a wound that will not heal up.

– Voss

If *The Tree of Man* is Genesis and the Book of Job, then *Voss* is Exodus and Ecclesiastes. Of course, Johann Ulrich Voss's desire to traverse the Australian continent in the middle of the nineteenth century is not equivalent to Moses leading his people to the Promised Land. If anything, hubris and the desire to possess a land that in its ancient vastness defies the comprehension and desires of one individual is at the heart of the novel: Voss, the explorer foreigner, annihilated but also liberated by his and our understanding that this obsession is impossible to realise, not only because the terrain resists such possession, but also because this land itself has already been crossed and recrossed by peoples with a history long preceding the European arrival in the "new world". However, *like* Moses in Exodus, Voss disappears from the narrative of this extraordinary novel. God's injunction refuses Moses his ultimate dream of arriving in the Promised Land. The God in this novel is the land itself; its unforgiving sternness and omnipotence is equivalent to the patriarchal Lord of the Jewish Bible.

The most exhilarating aspect of *Voss* is the communication that occurs between Voss and Laura Trevelyan, the young orphan who is the niece of Voss's benefactor, though they are physically separated by the inland journey that Voss makes. The novelist suspends realism so that the man and woman are in broken dialogue. As Voss's pride and certainty is undone by the savageness and isolation of his expedition, as his humiliation and terror finally result in his humbling, Laura comes to her own realisation that the attempt by the expatriated colonists to hold on to the materialistic aspirations and petty prejudices of bourgeois

England and Europe are another kind of human folly. Laura and Voss's mystical dialogue confirms the ancient truths revealed in that great ancient Jewish text Ecclesiastes: time, unfathomable time, mocks the dreams of all men and women. From there wisdom emerges.

Laura Trevelyan was perfectly at home in the environment to which she was no longer expected to belong. There were few by now who recognised her. New arrivals in the Colony, of whom invariably there seemed to be a preponderance, were unaware of her origins, and those who were safely established had too little thought for anything but their own success to point to an insignificant failure. This judgement of the world was received by Laura without shame. Indeed, she had discovered many compensations, for now that she was completely detached, she saw more deeply and more truthfully, and often loved what she saw, whether inanimate objects, such as a laborious plateful of pink meringues, or, in the case of human beings, a young wife striving with feverish elegance to disguise the presence of her unborn child.

– Voss

I finish *Voss* and I am exhausted. And elated. In a sense the novel is its own kind of folly – an attempt by a writer to attain imaginatively, in fiction, the revelatory power and immensity of an ancient myth.

Of course, it is by virtue of being outside history that myths retain their revelatory power. When myths are yoked to contemporary narratives and themes, there is always a tension between the elemental power of the mythology and the social and political exigencies of the present-day. There is therefore a danger in White's choice to make mythology out of the immense spiritual suffering and exaltation of both Voss and Laura.

I think the novel succeeds, even in its messiness, even at those points in the narrative where it is confused and overwrought, because White's pride and terror as a writer – *can I pull this great mad novel off?* – is an equivalent to Voss's own journey. But as a writer there is also something in his daring that I buck against, something that troubles me. I think it is that the mythic and spiritual dimensions of *Voss* are grander than the simplicity of *The Tree of Man*. It is as if Amy and Stan Parker are a *possible* Eve and Adam, and *possible* Jobs, in a fictional landscape in which we apprehend the potential for other Eves, other Adams and other Jobs – sensed, glimpsed, awaiting within the cosmology of the novel. But Voss and Laura dominate *Voss*; there is no other Voss in *Voss*, no other Laura, not even the whisper of an equivalent. More so than with the Parkers of *The Tree of Man*, we sense in *Voss* that from the consciousness of these characters the writer is attempting to forge a foundational myth of Australia.

I hope not to sound damning of White but today I find it impossible to commit to a foundational myth based on the experiences of two Europeans, no matter that they are outsiders to the colonial white world. So I am wary, I hold back from this novel. I can't imagine any non-Indigenous writer taking on the dare of *Voss* and committing to its equivalent in the present moment. The only Australian writers who can now follow on from this novel are Aboriginal writers. And it is no accident that the only Australian novels that I know that have dared this mythological grandeur since *Voss*, this weaving of history, myth, spirit and revelation, are Kim Scott's *Benang* (1999) and Alexis Wright's *Carpentaria* (2006). They are the novels that come closest to White's and that have gone beyond it.

'Go home, go home!' giggled and chanted the young girls.

'Go home to Germany!' sang the older women.

*There was a clapping and a stamping as the
men's chorus interpolated:*

'Go home! Go home! Go home to hell!'

*With a joyful, brassy resonance, because the
puppet in their lives had been replaced at last
by a man of flesh and blood.*

— Riders in the Chariot

If *Voss* is a dare I cannot wager, *Riders in the Chariot*
acts for me as a caution. This is a novel that I can
admire but it is one that I cannot love and I think
that has to do with how entrenched it is in the
politics and literary tropes of its time. Of all the
novels, stories and plays that White wrote in Castle
Hill, it is the one that most savagely dissects the
racism and pettiness of Australian culture. But the
very thing that I adore about White – his language
of the alien and the outsider, the migrant and
the foreigner – seems compromised here by him

so symbolically and purposefully making those themes manifest.

The novel consists of the voices of four characters: Miss Hare, an eccentric rich woman, Alf Dubbo, an Aboriginal artist, Ruth Godbold, a working-class washerwoman, and Mordecai Himmelfarb, a refugee and Holocaust survivor who has settled in Australia. Their stories are linked by each having a visionary experience of a chariot of fire, an image inspired by the Book of Ezekiel.

Though each character's voice and story has equal weight in the narrative, Himmelfarb's is undoubtedly central. His story culminates in his mock crucifixion in the yard of the factory in which he works. But it is as if in choosing to deal with the greatest outrage of the twentieth century, and in wanting to assert that the roots of such an outrage can be found in his own country, White had to abandon the physicality and sensuality that bring his best characters to life. Even as I write this I am conscious of being unfair: the writer's fury is just and righteous. And yet it is because Himmelfarb is such an overdetermined symbolic Christ figure that he does not quite convince as a human being.

It is ironic, given how fraught it is nowadays for a non-Indigenous author to write in an Aboriginal voice, that of all the characters in *Riders in the Chariot*, it is Alf Dubbo who is most visceral, most physical, who escapes the mid-twentieth century and can still challenge and move us in our present moment. Dubbo is a man wrenched from his Indigenous culture and isolated from the European world. Anger and alcohol, fear and animus are central to his life, and his fierce attempts to overcome his circumstances through a naïve but potent urge to be a painter are the book's most lacerating and effective passages. It is this combination of transcendence and self-destruction that most eloquently speaks to what a racist culture can do to a human being and it is, for me, this very combination that is denied Himmelfarb.

It is in this sense that *Riders in the Chariot* is a caution, as it illustrates how, when writers attempt to give imaginative shape and voice to our political concerns and furies, we might then find that our creations are overwhelmed by the inexorable rush of history; that contradictions that we are not yet aware of might return to undermine our work. In this case the outrage of the Holocaust butts up against the earlier but still existing outrage of European colonial usurpation of this continent's first peoples. One senses that White is grasping for such knowledge, and attempting to find a way to give expression to this clash of histories, but the equivalence given to Dubbo, Hare and Godbold now seems reductive. I think that for *Riders in the Chariot* to have transcended the moment of its writing, the twinning of Dubbo and Himmelfarb needed to have greater resonance, so that we were made *viscerally* aware of the obscene and ugly force of white Australia's resentment, fear and hatred of the Aborigine.

We feel the weight of the Australian fear of the immigrant and the Jew in the vivid and tragic moment of Himmelfarb's crucifixion. But it is as if White can't find the words to express the calamitous racism that defines white Australia's relationship to its first peoples. Or it might just be that from my vantage point in a new century, I feel I must issue this demand, despite knowing it is impossible for White to have answered it, writing at the end of the 1950s.

It was the kind of moment when Arthur sensed he would have to protect his brother, who was too clever by half, who read essays in class, who liked books, and who was said to be their mother's darling. Because of it all, Waldo needed defending from himself and others. It was all very well to hang on to your brother's hand because Waldo was accepted by the tight world, of tidiness and quick answers, of punctuality and unbreakable rules. Even Johnny Haynes and the boys who

went behind the dunnies to show what they'd got,
accepted Waldo by fits and starts, because they
were deceived, from some angles, into seeing him
as another of themselves. But poor Waldo was so
different, and so frail.

– The Solid Mandala

For all of White's visibility in later life as a vocal supporter of environmentalism, public funding for the arts, education and culture, for the union movement and the green bans, and against racism and Australia's involvement in the war in Vietnam, what I discover in his fiction is that he is not a political writer. Or rather, that the political is always woven silkily, tangentially and symbolically through his novels and short stories. From within the world of his stories what we can understand of struggle, of love, of sex, of poverty, of power, of life and of death, is only to be gleaned from the bold and vivid articulation and representation of the individual. White's fiction privileges doubt over surety and the iconoclast over the collective. It is the individual, and the individual as outsider, that is his most constant allegiance. That surge of imaginative commitment can only be understood as *existential*.

The Solid Mandala is a book that affirms for me the great potential still to be found in existential literature. It is as if, after committing to the grand narratives that are part of the righteous energy of *Riders in the Chariot* but also central to its heaviness as writing, White deliberately chose to work on a smaller canvas. But in Arthur and Waldo Brown, the twins who may embody White's hopes and fears for his own self, he has also given us one of the great works of fiction on the constant tension that every artist experiences: the tension between wishing to believe our commitment is to truth and courage, and our terror that we are in danger of acquiescing to greed and pride.

Both *Riders in the Chariot* and *The Solid Mandala* are set largely in Sarsaparilla, but the cruelty of insularity and convention has a much more potent force in the latter novel. What we discover in *The Solid Mandala* is that the suburban world can indeed be destructive to inspiration, that it can bind us to parochialism and spite. It does so for Waldo, who dreams of literary greatness but who lacks understanding and empathy and so ends up a deracinated and failed human being, destroyed by the very insular and suburban aspirations that he zealously denies in himself. And it is the child-man Arthur, who trusts in instinct, quiet and the goodness of the world – even if the world he traverses is not much bigger than Sarsaparilla itself – who lives in joy, precisely because he trusts in compassion and fellow-feeling.

In Waldo's arrogance and pride, I found a mirror of myself; his is ultimately an even more tragic pride than that of Voss, who is resurrected through his humiliation; whereas Waldo, in refusing to be humbled, is annihilated by it. And in Arthur's simplicity and kindness, I discovered how a writer might communicate the essence of spiritual compassion; how one might keep faith with the core truth of the Gospel writings and yet make such truth resonate for a secular, world-weary twenty-first century reader. In *The Solid Mandala* White compels us to look into the mirror by staring into that mirror himself: his reflection and our own become twinned, much as Waldo and Arthur are. It's a book that reminds us to be both brave and kind. And it is a book that, for a writer, inspires us not to be ashamed or fearful of the local and the particular and not to assume that cosmopolitanism is necessarily the antidote to parochialism. The cruel guardians of propriety, correctness and fashion are equally at home in the bush and in the metropolis. Sydney cannot redeem Waldo, for his vanity and resentment are with him wherever he goes. Whereas Arthur, who stays put, gains enlightenment. In *The Solid Mandala* the small, quiet town of Sarsaparilla becomes big enough to encompass all of the world.

So Arthur Brown danced, beginning at the first corner, from which he would proceed by stages to the fourth, and beyond. He who was so large, so shambly, found movement coming to him on the hillside in the bay of blackberries. The bands of his shirtsleeves were hanging open at his wrists. The bluish shadows in the less exposed parts of his skin, of his wrists, and the valley between his breasts, were soon pearled over.

In the first corner, as a prelude to all that he had to reveal, he danced the dance of himself. Half clumsy, half electric. He danced the gods dying on a field of crimson velvet, against the discord of human voices.

– The Solid Mandala

SYDNEY

*At Bangkok Madame de Lascabanes re-entered
her world.*

'Vous désirez, madame?'

'Rien, merci.' *It was actually true.*

*The Air France hostess had inquired so impersonally
that some (Australians for example, with their
manic insistence on 'warmth') might have judged
her contemptuous. Exchanging the ritual sliver of
a smile, the princess and the air hostess knew better.*

– The Eye of the Storm

Some time ago – exactly when I am not
sure, my recollection is hazy, memory
worn down by time – I was being driven
around Sydney by friends, and we were driving
past Centennial Park. "Where did Patrick White

and Manoly Lascaris live?" I asked. "Do you know?" My friend Jane pointed out the house. I asked her to stop the car and I went across the park and searched for some flowers. I picked and arranged a small bouquet of wild flowers, carefully tying them together with a long reed I snapped from where it was growing at the edge of a pond. From my back pocket I pulled out an old receipt and my pen, and on the back of the receipt I wrote the words "Thank you", and underneath the translation in Greek. I placed the bouquet and the note in the letterbox, went back to the car, got in, and said, "Okay, now we can drive off."

Patrick White must have already died and it is possible too that Lascaris had passed. I was leaving the message and the gift to their ghosts. I wanted to express my gratitude to both of them: to White for the books and plays and stories he had written; to Lascaris for giving White a greater knowledge of the world.

My inclusion of Lascaris in my gratitude is something I do in complete seriousness. In part it is because I don't think the acute and sensitive understanding that White has of the exile and of the migrant was possible without the writer's imaginative empathy with the experiences of his life partner. This understanding is, I think, one of his greatest gifts to the development of our national literature. By choosing to link his own personal and sexual alienation with the cultural isolation that he saw mirrored in the experience of the exile, White was able to create a literary language and a fluid and highly sensual writing that allowed him to move between genders and between states of being.

It might be, too, that in falling in love with Lascaris, and committing to a relationship that was to last until his death, White could live a homosexual life in Australia that might have been unbearable or only possible in the shadows if he were to have lived it alone. Ours was a deeply conservative country during the early and middle period of White's life. The larger metropolises of London, New York and Paris were enticing to generations of our artists who identified as sexual outsiders. Of course, I am indulging in speculation; but I am also confident that glimpses we find in Marr's biography and in White's own autobiography and letters support such speculation. I think he stayed in Australia for many reasons, but one of the central reasons was because of the life he and Manoly made here.

The Castle Hill years were a fertile source of inspiration for White's writing, and if there were moments when both he and Lascaris wished for the more tantalising and cosmopolitan pleasures of life in Europe or the USA, their decision to stay in Australia was, I think, profoundly right for his work. The very landscape fed both the real and the symbolic territories he created in *The Tree of Man*, in *Voss*, *Riders in the Chariot*, *The Solid Mandala* and in his short stories. It's possible too that his knowledge of the varied lives of the extended

Lascaris clan – across three continents – made him aware that to be forced into exile, or to exile oneself, meant that any return to an Australian homeland of the imagination would always be marked by nostalgia.

I wish to be careful here. I am not contending that White's greatness as a writer was conditional on his remaining in Australia but rather that it was *conditioned* by it. White's talents were liberated by the themes made possible to him as an intellectual and an artist in this country, resulting in a formal sensuousness and flourish. His example gives an ironic twist to our understanding of the "cultural cringe", a phenomenon he himself helped to define: it may well be that the writer from a colonial space faces greater danger in becoming an expatriate than in staying home.

All of us who have experience of growing up in migrant or refugee communities can bear witness to how the migrant's sense of origin is made traumatic by the past, and how the conception of homeland is seemingly embalmed by memory and history. Home is always the past and never the present. And I dare say many of us have had the experience of hearing writers who left Australia precisely because they believed that the possibilities were limited here, and yet everything they now write about their homeland shares in this sense of embalmment. Whereas everything that White has written seems real and present to us, even contemporary in its language and syntax. His is an Australian English. In its themes. In its surprising and intoxicating admixture of the elegant and the vulgar. In its humour. In its starkness. In its frustration. In its bodies. In its scents and sounds.

* * *

White and Lascaris sold Dogwoods in 1963 and moved to Sydney. By this time White's literary reputation was being cemented across the globe and it was also a time of greater immersion in the cultural life of his country. This is the time of his great friendship with Sidney Nolan and the beginning of his self-fashioning as the admonishing Jeremiah of Australian complacency and materialism. This is also the moment when Australian culture itself, particularly in Sydney, is beginning to shrug off its colonial dependency on Mother Britain, and where the stirrings from bohemian, artistic and student circles will lead to a transformation of the city. Cultural change emerged not only from within these bourgeois circles – this is also the period when the deadening and corrosive edifice of the White Australia Policy was being challenged by the hundreds of thousands of Jewish, Eastern and Southern European migrants arriving in Australia and making their homes in our cities. It is no wonder this new, changing Sydney beckoned.

These changes, these stirrings, will take time to coalesce into the great wave that swept the Whitlam Labor Government into power in 1972 and shattered the decades-long hegemony of conservative rule and censorious culture. The novel that White will write during the late sixties and release at the end of the decade, *The Vivisector*, will be a harbinger of this wave. It will also feature three of my favourite characters in White's oeuvre: the painter Hurtle Duffield, his sister Rhoda, and his sophisticated and world-weary mistress, Hero Pavloussi.

For me, the most electric passages in *Riders in the Chariot* are the descriptions of the brutal canvases that Dubbo paints in his attempt to make material the knowledge he had received in his sublime vision of the chariot. In *The Vivisector* White's love of the activity and art of painting dominates the whole novel; it is as if all the writer wishes to express about the work of the imagination and the ferocious need to translate spiritual and emotional experience is communicated through the life of the artist Duffield. White found through his admiration of painting a means by which to elucidate that most slippery and well-nigh impossible subject: what is the alchemy by which imagination takes material form? How does it become concrete and manifest? Writing of the physical and material exertions of painting – the holding of the brush, the outlining of one's subject, the shaping of form and the mixing of oils, the laying of colour on the canvas, the immersion in the painting itself and then the stepping away from it – enabled him to explore metaphor, analogy and symbol in a way that might not be possible if he had made his artist a writer. The sensuality and physicality that is as integral to White's writing as his phenomenal control over the English language is vividly expressed in the novel. The privileging of the outsider and the exquisitely forensic understanding of the psychology of the exile are here as well; not only in the artist himself, but also in Rhoda and Hero. And here too is the wrestling with the sin of pride: for all of Duffield's success in the world, he must come to an understanding of the threat that his ego and desire for success pose to the integrity of his work. It is impossible not to see authorial self-reflection at work in this novel. Duffield's ultimate awareness of his limitations as both a man and an artist is not resolved in the fury of destruction that overcame Dubbo in *Riders of the Chariot*: an accommodation is ultimately reached. I read *The Vivisector* as a novel proclaiming that White is, if not content, at least coming to peace with his status and his place as a writer in the world.

If I have learnt anything of importance, it was you who taught me, and I thank you for it [. . .] It was you who taught me how to see, to be, to know instinctively. When I used to come to your house in Flint Street, melting with excitement and terror wondering how I would dare go through with it again, or whether I would turn to wood, or dough, or say something so stupid and tactless you would chuck me out into the street, it wasn't simply the thought of the delicious kisses and all the other play which forced the courage in me. It was the paintings I used to look at sideways whenever

I got the chance. I wouldn't have let on because I was afraid you might have been amused and made me talk about them, and been even more amused when I couldn't discuss them at your level. But I was drinking them in through the pores of my skin.

– The Vivisector

The Vivisector is White's longest novel and it has an assured structure; it never lags, meanders or seems overwrought. Considering its subject is the meaning of artistic expression, that is an astounding feat. Although written almost fifty years ago, it suggests a way out of the cul-de-sac of self-referential introspection which can mar so many novels that make the writer and writing the means through which to examine an imaginative life. We writers love writing but we must also love music and painting and film and sport – whatever the medium is that can give the reader insight into the work of the imagination. In *The Vivisector* these insights are communicated through painting.

Yet it is the next novel that White writes that is forever now in my blood and in my soul as a reader – a third novel, after *The Tree of Man* and *The Solid Mandala*, that dumbfounds me with its structural coherence, its illumination of life and family and class, its insights into aspiration and pride, regret and age. This is *The Eye of the Storm*, and with this novel, set in contemporary Sydney, it is as if White has come to a point where he can honestly dissect the privileged social world from which he comes.

Elizabeth Hunter is reaching the end of her life, still living in her grand mansion in Sydney, being cared for day and night by two nurses, with occasional visits by her long-time lawyer, whose reticent love for her has been constant for decades. In preparation for her death, her two children have returned to Australia. Sir Basil is an actor of diminishing talent, and Dorothy de Lascabares has married into a dissolute French aristocratic family.

Even from such a cursory outline it must be evident that the novel is, in part, a satire. Basil and Dorothy are exiles, but their condition lacks the human nobility granted mad but ultimately enlightened Theodora in *The Aunt's Story;* or the dignity given to Voss in his wrestling with pride and his ultimate submission to death; or the dignity achieved through grace and acquiescence to nature and time by the Parkers in *The Tree of Man*. Basil and Dorothy lack the compassion that allows the seers of *Riders in the Chariot* and Arthur Brown in *The Solid Mandala* to understand that there exists another world that is not bound by the insularity, meanness and selfishness that is Sarsaparilla. And even though Sir Basil is an artist himself, he has settled for glittering prizes and the deprecation of his art; unlike Duffield, he has betrayed his talents and his opportunities. I cannot help but read this as a corrosive and explosively funny lampooning of the expat bourgeois Australian. Basil and Dorothy have abandoned a country that they sneer at as provincial and uncultured, only to settle for the most redundant and ignoble of goals by which to justify their exile – in his case a knighthood, in hers an attachment to a derelict and now meaningless European royal title. As contemporary readers we might mock aspirations redolent of a receding colonial past, but the sting in the tail of the novel is the reminder it gives of how many of us are still panting after such acknowledgement by the "real world" outside Australia, those equally redundant baubles, be they an Academy Award, a Booker Prize, a Commonwealth Prize, those still endlessly coveted bloody knighthoods and OBEs.

Or a Nobel Prize in literature. The novel will be published on the eve of White's winning this most prestigious of literary prizes, and for all his scoffing and proclaimed lack of interest in the honour, it is clear that his indifference was feigned. Gaining that honour meant much to him, not least that it was an achievement he could throw in the faces of the local critics who he believed had always misunderstood and misrepresented his writing. What did their opinion matter when the world had placed him in the pantheon of twentieth-century greats? Yet *The Eye of the Storm* itself was written just before the prize was awarded. It is a clue that his critique of such prizes was not wholly disingenuous. Sir Basil and Dorothy are pathetic in the poverty of their preening and self-congratulation, but they are never simple caricatures. We recognise ourselves in them. The cultural cringe has no better expression than in this novel, and its power is such that it can still be felt as a slap in the face many decades later.

The Eye of the Storm is as epic as *Voss*; the psychical topography it traverses is as grand and as overwhelming as the physical landscape of that earlier novel. What is most audacious and expert in the novel is the seamless movement in and out of the consciousness of its varied characters.

This is one of White's central strengths as a writer, and his ability to allow a narrative to speak as a chorus without ever losing control of individual voices reaches an apotheosis in *The Eye of the Storm*. I believe this is why my Filipina writer friend responded so immediately and joyously to the novel. She felt what I also experienced on reading it: the potential for fiction to break through the barriers of temporality and space – to be simultaneously historic and contemporary. To achieve this within the frame of what might be considered a "domestic novel" (the bulk of the action takes place in the decaying family mansion, and the house too has its own distinct, thrilling voice), reveals the poverty of such critical distinctions.

But the greatest creation in *The Eye of the Storm* is the dying grand dame, Elizabeth Hunter. She anchors the narrative, she is the prima donna around which the various operatic arias of the novel coalesce. That she is also vain, imperious, cruel and selfish does not in any way impede our ecstatic immersion in her voice and story. There is the temptation to read Elizabeth as autobiography, to write White's public and biographical persona into the character. Vanity, imperiousness, cruelty and selfishness. But such a temptation is also reductive and cannot contain all that Elizabeth is. Rather than the labouring Parkers, the suburban world of the Browns or the bohemian Sydney of Duffield, in this novel White is painting the city and the country his mother came from and the haute bourgeois world she inhabited. The world that produced him, as well.

If Elizabeth Hunter is monstrous, she is also granted spiritual transcendence, that glimpse into the chaos and order at the heart of human experience that is granted to Stan Parker, to Arthur Brown, to all the characters in *Riders in the Chariot*, and ultimately to Voss as he lies dying. We are there with Elizabeth as she experiences this searing vision at the island on which she is holidaying as the wild tempest emerges from the great ocean.

In the stillness of the storm's eye. As always in White, this unveiling is only momentary, before Elizabeth is returned to herself. She remains selfish and cruel but that moment lasts a lifetime and that vision is there with her at the hour of her death. No, I am wrong – it is a mistake to conceive of Elizabeth as monstrous. There are no monsters in White. Though he borrows signs and meanings from Christianity, Orthodox and Protestant, and from Judaism, White's spiritual vision is also Pagan.[2] Vision can be granted to the kind and the unkind alike.

---

2 Only recently did I realise that the title of The Burnt Ones is a translation of the Greek phrase "οι καμένοι", meaning literally "those who are burnt". This title, too, must be another gift from Lascaris. It is an expression of White's deep yet Pagan faith, his allegiance to those who suffer and to those who are outsiders; his love is for those abandoned or condemned to Hell, to the fire.

Without much thought for her own wreckage,
she moved slowly down what had been a beach,
picking her way between torn-off branches, great
beaded hassocks of amber week, everywhere fish
the sea had tossed out, together with a loaf of no
longer bread, but a fluffier, disintegrating foam
rubber. Just as she was no longer a body, least of
all a woman: the myth of her womanhood had
been exploded by the storm. She was instead
a being, or more likely a flaw at the centre of
this jewel of light: the jewel itself, blinding and
tremulous at the same time, existed, flaw and
all, only by grace; for the storm was still visibly
spinning and boiling at a distance, in columns
of cloud, its walls hung with vaporous balconies,
continually shifted and distorted.

– The Eye of the Storm

RETURNING HOME

*The women continued sitting side by side, till
Eadie found the strength to rummage in her bag,
and when she had found the pencil she was looking
for, to scribble on the prayer-book's fly-leaf.*

*Eadith was offered this tremulous scribble, and
read, 'Are you my son Eddie?'*

*They were seated on this other bench inside the
corrugated-iron shelter, sun glazing on black
asphalt as the brown, bucking tram approached
them.*

*'I do wish, Eddie, you'd stop picking that scab on
your knee. Sometimes I think you do things just to
irritate me.'*

*'Sometimes I think, Mother, you hate just about
everything I do.'*

Now in this violet, northern light, purged of her mortal sins by age, Eadie might have been prepared to accept a bit of scab-picking in others.

If Eadith could have unbent. But if she had, she might have broken. At least she couldn't have trusted her lips.

Instead, she seized the pecil and slashed the fly-leaf of the prayer-book with a savagery she did not feel.

Eadie Twyborn read when the book was handed back, 'No, but I am your daughter Eadith.'

The two women continued sitting together in the gathering shadow.

Presently Eadie said, 'I am so glad. I've always wanted a daughter.'

– The Twyborn Affair

I t is 2017 and it is the fortnight of the Melbourne Writers Festival. I am at one of those parties high on the thirty-fifth floor of an international hotel, and the narrow conference room is crammed with writers, agents, publicists and publishers. I am getting nicely and woozily drunk. I find myself at the edge of a circle that is nodding approvingly as an English writer loudly criticises those morons who voted for Brexit. Her assumption is that all of us listening share her politics and prejudices.

Fortified by three glasses of wine, I make an objection. I remind her of an earlier referendum held in Europe, the one in Greece where the population overwhelmingly voted against the austerity project of the European Union. I get admittedly emotional as I point out that the wishes of this part of Europe were ignored. Maybe, I argue, not every Brexit vote is attributable to racism and xenophobia, maybe they are right to be suspicious of the EU. The woman hears me out with that cool politeness that is the birthright of the English upper class, and then continues with her righteous lecture as if she had never been interrupted. One of the Australians in the circle grants me a furtive and warm wink, but everyone knows on which side their festival bread is buttered and I skulk away.

I put a cigarette to my mouth and am about to take the lift down to the ground floor when I hear my name being called. It's an old friend, a wonderful poet and writer, and he grabs me and gives me a massive bear hug. I vent to him about "the fucking English" and we exchange stories about how even after all this time just one withering look or comment by some North London snob can somehow manage to put us in our colonial place. He is as Australian as I am, with Muslim and South-East Asian heritage, and we joke about how in Australia, while we are always upfront and vocal in our fury at our nation's racism and parochialism, when it comes to being in England and hearing our country criticised we find ourselves on the defensive, even making excuses for our wretched history. We fall about laughing at the absurdity that we often find ourselves defending Australia while our Anglo-Australian writer friends join in the chorus of derision. And that's when he makes a point, perceptive and troubling: You know, Christos, he says, it's because we can't write in our mother tongues, we have to write in English, and so as writers Australia is the only home we can have.

And I tell him about my year spent reading Patrick White, of my discovery and rediscovery of White as a writer. Of how White gave expression and clarity to the point he has just made. Of how I discovered that Patrick White has been the first of our writers to represent the migrant experience. He looks at me quizzically. You sure? Yeah, I answer, Read him.

And in the lift, hurtling down, I am reminded of the man's question at that festival in Cheltenham, What do Australians now think of Patrick White?

And, in this empty lift, I call out an answer: I love him. And my *pissed-offness*: at my own failures, at my own cultural cringe, at my own hubris in wanting to take the weight of my continent's failures on my feeble shoulders – it vanishes for a moment. Only for a moment. And I express a wish, a hope, that I will one day write something worthy as a gift for him. I touch wood, I touch it three times for the vanity of such a hope. The lift doors open and the world rushes back in.

*　*　*

When did I first fall in love with White? Why did I wish to place a gift of flowers at his gate? In this journey of reading him, reading all his novels, rereading all his stories, I left *The Twyborn Affair* to the end. I did this because I recalled the delirious excitement I felt as a young man reading this shape-shifting story of Eddie/Eadith Twyborn, the highborn colonial boy who goes from being a jackeroo to the madam of a brothel in England.

I put *The Twyborn Affair* aside until last because of my trepidation at returning to a novel that I had held in my heart so closely and dearly for so many years. But from the opening lines I understood that my fears were unwarranted. Set in an Australia I hardly recognised, an Australia not yet transformed by the immigration that would transfigure the nation, the novel unfurls in a jubilant dance of sentences that are at every point marked by the sensual: the way bodies move, the way bodies sweat, the way bodies fuck, the way bodies fail. It is a novel about a trans woman that is queer *avant-la-lettre*, and also a novel that remains contemporary even as it speaks to us in a language and form that we recognise as coming from the past. Is this a contradiction? Possibly. But I am no longer the young man I was when I first read the novel, and such contradictions no longer necessarily trouble me. This acceptance of contradiction is also one of the great gifts literature has granted me.

The Twyborn Affair is a reminder that the best fiction evades containment and precise borders, neat summations and formulaic critical categories. Eadith is one of White's exiles, one of his greatest creations, and re-reading the novel I am reminded that I am sometimes in danger of confusing rawness with authenticity. That formidable control and elegance in White's style reaches such astonishing heights in this late period, the period of both *The Eye of the Storm* and *The Twyborn Affair*, that we can overlook a perversity that has always been there in his writing. By "perversity" I mean a going against the grain that is alive not only to the spiritual and existential condition of being an outsider, but also to the pleasures and erotics of such a condition. It is there in his script for *The Night the Prowler*, that gloriously demented film about the sexual and emotional release that can be found in transgression. The émigré and the transgressor both: the heroes, always, of White's fiction.

And there you have it. Patrick White, accused of misogyny and misanthropy but the writer of some of the greatest female characters in our fiction. Patrick White, the child of a long-vanished squattocratic past, whose sympathy lay with the migrant and the outsider and who made these outsiders the centre of his fiction. Patrick White, frequently castigated as chaste and suspicious of the sexual freedoms unleashed by feminism and gay liberation, but whose writing from the very beginning, right from *The Happy Valley*, is potent with the thrill of the erotic. Patrick White, the un-Australian writer who did more than any other writer in the twentieth century to create an imaginative language that we can call Australian, who unshackled us from the demand that we write as the English do, who recognised, through his own alienation and also through his profound love for his partner, that we were a migrant and mongrel nation forging our own culture and our own language.

Thank you, Mr White. And thank you, Mr Lascaris. *Ευχαριστώ.*

Christos Tsiolkas, 2018

WORKS BY PATRICK WHITE

NOVELS

Happy Valley (1939)

The Living and the Dead (1941)

The Aunt's Story (1948)

The Tree of Man (1955)

Voss (1957)

Riders in the Chariot (1961)

The Solid Mandala (1966)

The Vivisector (1970)

The Eye of the Storm (1973)

A Fringe of Leaves (1976)

The Twyborn Affair (1979)

Memoirs of Many in One (1986)

The Hanging Garden (2012, posthumous)

SHORT STORY COLLECTIONS
The Burnt Ones (1964)
The Cockatoos (1974)
Three Uneasy Pieces (1987)

POETRY
Thirteen Poems (under the pseudonym
Patrick Victor Martindale, c. 1929)
The Ploughman and Other Poems (1935)
Poems (1974)

PLAYS
Bread and Butter Women (1935, unpublished)
The School for Friends (1935, unpublished)
Return to Abyssinia (1948, unpublished)
The Ham Funeral (1947)
The Season at Sarsaparilla (1962)
A Cheery Soul (1963)
Night on Bald Mountain (1964)
Big Toys (1977)

*Signal Driver: A Morality Play
for the Times* (1982)
Netherwood (1983)
Shepherd on the Rocks (1987)

SCREENPLAY

The Night the Prowler (1978)

AUTOBIOGRAPHY

Flaws in the Glass (1981)